SCALE OF STATUTE MILES

NATURAL SCALE = 1:200...

Reference *Astronomical positions*

Boundary Lines — — —
shewn coloured thus —·—·—~·—/ *Boundary mark on M.t Rorai*

Astronomical Positions

NAME OF PLACE	LATITUDE.N.	LONGITUDE W OF GREENWICH	AUTHORITY	NAME OF PLACE	LATITUDE.N.	LONGITUDE.W OF GREENWICH
Punta Playa	8 33 22	59 59 48·5	1st Expedition	Camp 3 Cuyuni River	6 49 28·9	60 39 12·8
Mururuma River M.th	8 18 44	59 48 10	,, ,,	Camp 4 ,, ,,	6 47 04·8	60 46 36·3
Boundary Mark do	8 19 00	59 48 22·7	,, ,,	Ekereku River Mouth	6 43 02·8	60 56 23·7
Mururuma River H.d	8 14 05·3	59 50 07·9	,, ,,	Wenamu River ,,	6 42 40·9	61 08 00·7
Haiowa River M.th	8 13 04	59 56 39·1	n ,,	Pathawaru Wenamu R	6 28 02·3	61 07 54·1
La Lancha, Amacura R	8 02 18	60 05 00	,, ,,	Arawai Fall ,,	6 19 36·5	61 09 22·7
San Victor, ,,	7 58 42	60 10 05·5	,, ,,	Tshuau Village ,,	6 11 45·8	61 07 22·1
La Horqueta, ,,	7 52 18·2	60 18 22	,, ,,	Kura Falls ,,	6 03 42·5	61 16 46·6
Amacura River H.d	7 49 00	60 21 53·1	,, ,,	Dead Man's Camp ,,	5 58 06	61 22 55·7
Harrison Falls Barima R	7 38 24	60 20 37·8	2nd Expedition	W.most source Wenamu R.	5 56 55·4	61 23 24·7
Five Star Camp ,,	7 35 37	60 23 13·8	,, ,,	Paruima River Camp	5 51 01·7	61 03 08·1
Kaliaku Camp ,,	7 33 19	60 37 07·5	,, ,,	Kamarang ,, ,,	5 43 37·2	61 04 15·5
Barima River Head	7 28 24	60 41 31·2	,, ,,	Arrive Matai	5 36 35	61 21 15·3
Akarabisi River Head	7 08 27·7	60 20 51·1	,, ,,	Yuruani River	5 11 00	80 58 36·5
,, Mouth	6 55 47·1	60 22 01·7	3rd Expedition	Kamaiwawong Village	5 10 11·1	60 41 45·3
Camp 2 Cuyuni River	6 51 32·3	60 32 21·5	,, ,,	Boundary Mark Mount	5 10 09·6	60 45 58·2

IMPERIAL AMBITION

Venezuela's Threat to Guyana

An Indictment of Guyana's Western Neighbour

Ministry of Foreign Affairs and
International Cooperation, Guyana

First published in 2021 by Hansib Publications

info@hansibpublications.com
www.hansibpublications.com

Hansib Publications Ltd
76 High Street, Hertford, Herts, SG14 3TA, UK

ISBN 978-1-912662-43-2
ISBN 978-1-912662-44-9 (Kindle)
ISBN 978-1-912662-45-6 (ePub)

Front cover image, *Dawn on Roraima: Guyana's western
border*, copyright © Jonathan Wilkins

A CIP catalogue record for this book
is available from the British Library

Produced by Hansib Publications Limited

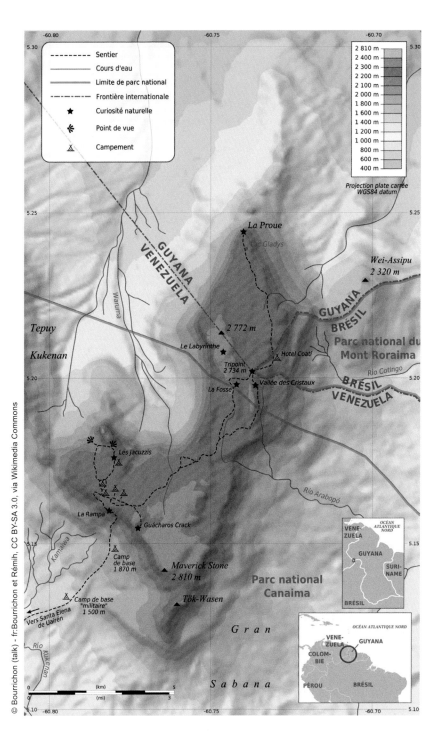

Mt. Roraima: The Tri-Junction Boundary

The Arbitral Tribunal and Counsel, Paris 1899

Contents

Foreword 11

PART I

A Shameful Quest 15
Self-determination 16
The Treaty of Washington, 1897 16
The Arbitral Tribunal 19
Venezuela applauds the Award 20
Demarcation of the Boundary 21
Venezuela protects the Boundary 22
The Tri-Junction Point 24
Venezuelan greed revived 28
The Mallet-Prevost stratagem 30
The 'Cold War' dimension 32
The 'David and Goliath' torment 34
The Geneva Agreement, 1966 35
Fifty years of Venezuelan 'filibuster' 37
Destroying International Agreements 38
The Sanctity of Treaties 42
Rogue States 43

PART II

A clear path to 'judicial settlement' 47
S.G. Ban Ki-moon's 'Way Forward' 48
Four Secretaries-General 49

Guyana's Full Cooperation 50
Venezuelan Militarism Paramount 51
Venezuela rejects 'Confidence Building' 51
Bilateral Meetings Falter 51
The Meaning of 'Significant Progress' 52
"Moving Forward" 53
The Secretary-General 'chooses' 55
Oral Hearing on 30 June 2020 56
The Court's Jurisdiction 57
Venezuela's Outrage 59
We are not Alone 61
Venezuela's Opposition to Legal Process 63
The 'Justice' of the 1899 Award 66
The Cleveland Commission 66
The 'Paris' Tribunal 68
A Unanimous Decision 68
Venezuelan 'Injustice' 69
'Justice' twice fulfilled 70

Foreword

"We cannot recall the moment of Guyana's Independence without also remembering the efforts of Venezuela to prevent it. As we released ourselves from the colonial cord of Britain, the Venezuelan government sought to stifle our birth by falsely laying claim to two-thirds of our country.

They have spent the last fifty-five years of the independence of all of Guyana in pursuing this claim - but international law is not silent. The International Court of Justice is the forum where the voice of international law will be heard and justice will be determined.

As one people, with one united voice, and a spirit that will not be broken, we will advance the validity of the 122-year-old Award that fixed our boundaries.

In our continuing struggle, we are not without friends. We deeply appreciate all those who have stood by our side – from the Caribbean, from the Commonwealth, from the Americas and beyond.

The Venezuelans must understand that we sought no quarrel with them, and we do not do so now. Our only wish is to live in harmony and cooperation with all our neighbours. We hold out not a fist of war but a hand of friendship, based on respect for our borders and theirs.

But we will not be cowered, nor will we be bullied."

So said Guyana's President, His Excellency Dr Irfaan Ali, in addressing the people of Guyana on 26th May 2021 – the 55th anniversary of the Independence of the Cooperative Republic Guyana.

This booklet is in furtherance of Guyana's defence of its sovereignty. It is called *IMPERIAL AMBITION: Venezuela's Threat to Guyana*. It elaborates the themes to which the President spoke when marking the self-determination of the people of Guyana fifty-five years ago.

On the 50th Anniversary of Guyana's Independence in 2016, its Government issued *The New Conquistadors: The Venezuelan Challenge to Guyana's Sovereignty*. In this successor publication, the mask of the conquistador is stripped off, revealing the naked visage of Venezuelan imperialism and its ambition to possess two-thirds of Guyana.

This booklet is in two Parts: Part I, updating *The New Conquistadors* and Part II enlarging its coverage into the phase of more active United Nations involvement and that of the International Court of Justice. Its purpose is to inform the people of Guyana, the Caribbean region and the international community more widely of the shameful imperial quest that drives the Venezuelan threat to Guyana.

The photograph on the front cover is of the prow of Mt. Roraima on whose historic summit the boundaries of Guyana, Venezuela and Brazil intersect – the 'tri-junction point'. That 'boundary point' was formally marked with a pyramid in 1931 by an official Mixed Commission of the three countries. It was the commencement of the demarcation of the Guyana-Brazil boundary on the Guyana-Venezuela boundary line, as explained at pages 24-7 below.

Mt. Roraima is a reminder for all time and to all people of Venezuela's eastern border. Guyana's sun sets there – on Mt. Roraima – and always will.

**Ministry of Foreign Affairs and International Cooperation,
Georgetown
1 June 2021**

Part I

Imperial Ambition

O n Guyana's north-western shore – the Essequibo Coast – is Shell Beach. It is the quintessence of Guyana itself in its need for protection of the new born turtles that rise from its golden sands only to battle their way to survival past predators in their path. Guyana's first years have been like the first hazardous moments of our turtles. And as it is with them, it has been and remains the world's responsibility to secure new-born countries like Guyana from the predators that would devour them. The world seeks to discharge that responsibility essentially by international law. It is by violating international law that others on their frontiers try to despoil them of the right to survival that is their patrimony. So has it been with

Newborn turtles at Shell Beach, Essequibo

Guyana. And as fifty years are but an hour in a nation's life, that threat to survival persists as Guyana celebrated the 50th Anniversary of its Independence on 26 May 2016, and of its becoming the Cooperative Republic of Guyana on 23 February 2020.

Self-determination

Decolonisation is for many the greatest achievement of the post-war world, and Guyana's Independence was a part of it. It was a process of self-determination welcomed by most freedom loving people and Governments. But the welcome of Guyana's freedom was not shared by the Government of its neighbour to the west who, ironically, was to call their country the *Bolivarian Republic of Venezuela*. That singular aversion to Guyana's freedom was the very converse of all that Simon Bolivar symbolises. And it was not resentment alone that Venezuela nurtured. In anti-Bolivarian fashion, Venezuela actually tried to obstruct Guyana's Independence – to prevent the start of the last fifty-five years. This could not be the wish or the work of our brothers and sisters in Venezuela, the ordinary people of our neighbouring land. They are neighbours against whom the people of Guyana nurture no ill will. But there are classes and forces in Venezuela that have made the acquisition of most of Guyana their life's cause, and sought to turn it into a national crusade. Venezuela is already the fifth largest country of South America, with Guyana among the smallest. The numbers are eloquent; Venezuela is 353,841 square miles; Guyana is 83,000 square miles. The Venezuelan crusade is to further widen that disparity by stripping Guyana of the Essequibo Region – almost three quarters of the country.

The Treaty of Washington, 1897

In 1962, four years before Guyana's Independence, the then Venezuelan Government had taken advantage of Guyana's pending freedom to try to reopen with Britain a long-settled border controversy involving almost three-quarters of Guyana's land area. It was a spurious and, in some ways, a sinister scheme to rob Guyana of its patrimony. In its outturn, three months before Guyana's Independence, in early 1966, Britain invited the 'about to be independent' Guyana to join in its conversations with Venezuela in the hope that the new country could be rid of Venezuelan greed at birth.

The outcome was the Geneva Agreement of 1966 between Venezuela and the United Kingdom, to which on attaining independence, Guyana became a party 'in addition to' Britain. It was Guyana's first international foray; and but for Venezuela's unwarranted intervention in the self-determination process, should not have been necessary – for British Guiana's boundary with Venezuela had been formally settled over sixty years previously by an International Tribunal of Arbitration under a Treaty freely signed by Venezuela and ratified by its Congress: the Treaty of Washington 1897. The 1962 attempt to undo history signalled a Venezuelan land-grab – a shameful crusade of greed.

President Joaquin Crespo commending the Treaty of Washington to the Venezuelan Congress on 20 February 1897 for ratification:

"It is eminently just to recognise the fact that the great republic (the United States of America) has strenuously endeavoured to conduct this matter in the most favourable way, and the result obtained represents an effort of intelligence and good will worthy of praise and thanks from us who are so intimately acquainted with the conditions of this most complicated question. It is your duty according to the constitutional law of the republic to examine the treaty which the Venezuelan Minister Plenipotentiary signed in accordance with the bases referred to and the change proposed by the executive power in regard to the formation of the arbitral tribunal. And as this is an affair of such importance involving as it does such sacred interests, I beg you that from the moment it is presented for your consideration you will postpone all other business until you shall decide upon it." (Translation)

Venezuela had long cast envious eyes on the Essequibo region of Guyana – almost two-thirds of its neighbour's land. Britain had claimed in turn the Orinoco Delta of Venezuela. It was the days of the *Monroe Doctrine* and the United States of America, acting as Venezuela's patron, had pressured Britain at Venezuelan insistence into agreeing to signing a Treaty of Arbitration with Venezuela under threat of war – so fierce was America's hemispheric posture. That was 2nd February 1897. It was a Treaty to settle for all time the boundary between Venezuela and Britain's colony of British Guiana. Venezuela and Britain undertook in solemn terms *"to consider the results of the proceeds of the Tribunal of Arbitration as a full, perfect and final settlement of all the questions referred to the Arbitrators."*

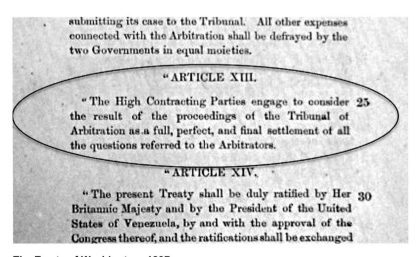

The Treaty of Washington, 1897

The Arbitral Tribunal

Venezuela claimed that they were the heirs of Spanish colonialism and that Spain had occupied more than half of the British colony before the British came. The Tribunal went into the most elaborate examination of the history of the occupation of the territory. The arguments took four hours each day, four days each week and occupied a period of nearly three months. The verbatim records of the hearings fill 54 printed volumes – with cases and counter-cases, and additional documents, correspondence and evidence. The Tribunal was presided over by M. de Martens, Professor of International Law at the University of St Petersburg, perhaps the most eminent international lawyer of the time. The other judges were: on the part of Venezuela, US Chief Justice Weston Fuller, nominated by the President of Venezuela; Justice David Josiah Brewer, of the US Supreme Court, nominated by the President of the United States and, on the part of Great Britain, Lord Russell of Killowen (Lord Chief Justice of England) and Sir Richard Henn Collins, a Lord Justice of Appeal of the English High Court. It is these four Judges that together chose Professor de Martens as the President of the Tribunal.

Rules of Procedure of the Tribunal of Arbitration, Rule XXIV

"The final award, duly declared and communicated to the Agents of the two Governments being in dispute shall be deemed to decide definitely the points in dispute between the Governments of Great Britain and of The United States of Venezuela concerning the lines of their respective frontiers, and shall finally close all Proceedings of the Tribunal of Arbitration established by the Treaty of Washington."

Venezuela applauds the Award

On 3 October 1899, the International Tribunal of Arbitration presented its Award. In the words of the law firm handling Venezuela's case, written in the American Journal of International Law as late as 1949: *"The Award secured to Venezuela the mouth of the Orinoco and control of the Orinoco basin, these being the most important questions at issue"*. Britain was awarded the less 'important' underdeveloped rest. It was a success for Venezuela; the law firm used the prestigious Journal's account of the Award to adorn its credentials. Their exuberance was not without reason. In the days following the Award, on 7 October 1899, Venezuela's Ambassador to Britain, Jose Andrade – the brother of the then Venezuelan President – commented: *We were given the exclusive dominion over the Orinoco, which was the principle aim we sought to achieve through arbitration.*

The justice of the Award

Sr. Andrade, Venezuelan Minister to London, 7 October 1899

"Greatly indeed did justice shine forth when, in spite of all, in the determining of the frontier the exclusive dominion of the Orinoco was granted to us, which is the principal aim which we set ourselves to obtain through arbitration. I consider well spent the humble efforts which I devoted personally to this end during the last six years of my public life."

Two months after the Award the American President William McKinley (Venezuela's patron) confirmed the mood of satisfaction in Caracas – in his State of the Union Message to Congress on 5 December 1899.

President McKinley's State of the Union Message to Congress, 5 December 1899

"The International Commission of Arbitration appointed under The Anglo-Venezuelan Treaty of 1897 rendered an award on October 3 last whereby the boundaries line between Venezuela and British Guiana is determined; thus ending a controversy which had existed for the greater part of the century. The award, as to which the Arbitrators were unanimous, while not meeting the extreme contention of either party, gives to Great Britain a large share of the interior territory in dispute and to Venezuela the entire mouth of the Orinoco, including Barima Point and the Caribbean littoral for some distance to the eastwards. The decision appears to be equally satisfactory to both parties."

Demarcation of the Boundary

As required by the Treaty and the Award, the boundary as determined by the Award was demarcated on the ground between 1900 and 1904 by Commissioners appointed by Britain and Venezuela. For Venezuela, the Commissioners were Dr Abraham Tirado, Civil Engineer of the United States of Venezuela and Chief of the Boundary Commission and Dr Elias Toro, Surgeon General of 'the Illustrious Central University of Venezuela' and Second Commissioner on behalf of Venezuela. On 7 January 1905, an official boundary map delineating the boundary as awarded and demarcated was drawn up, signed by Dr Tirado and Dr Toro, and by the British Commissioners H.J. Perkins and C. Wilgress Anderson, and promulgated in Georgetown at the Combined Court.

The Report submitted to the Venezuelan Government by Dr Tirado, the head of the Venezuelan Boundary Commissioners, speaks volumes of Venezuelan recognition and satisfaction with the Treaty, the Award and the Map – as the closing words of his report conveyed.

Dr Tirado's Report Forwarding the Official Boundary Map

The honourable task is ended and the delimitation between our Republic and the Colony of British Guiana an accomplished fact.

I, satisfied with the part which it has been my lot to play, congratulate Venezuela in the person of the patriotic Administrator who rules her destinies and who sees with generous pride the long-standing and irritating dispute that has caused his country so much annoyance settled under his regime.

Abraham Tirado
March 20, 1905

Venezuela protects the Boundary

That this was no pretence of respect for the Award and the related delimitation was well borne out in 1911 in replacing the Marker at the northernmost point of the Boundary (Punta Playa) when it was found to be washed away. Venezuela insisted that the replacement be strictly in accord with the 1899 Paris Award. The then President of Venezuela specifically authorised the undertaking.

General Juan Vicente Gomez
President of the US of Venezuela

WHEREAS I confer FULL POWERS that in his capacity a Commissioner following the instructions given will proceed to replace the post which was washed away by the sea in the extreme of the frontier between Venezuela and British Guiana

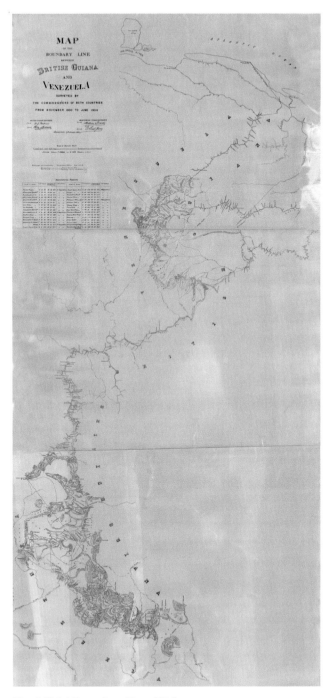

The Official Boundary Map, 1905

at Punta Playa with another which necessarily will be placed at the precise point where the boundary line cut now the line fixed in nineteen hundred in accordance with the Award signed at Paris the 3rd of October by the Mixed Commission Anglo-Venezuelan.

(Sgd) J. V. Gomez
Translation (sgd) Antonio G. Monagas
Consul for the U.S. of Venezuela

It was the boundary as shown on that definitive map of 1905, authenticated with pride by their Minister of Internal Relations, F. Alientaro, that the then Venezuelan Government used to celebrate their first one hundred years of Independence in 1911. A century and five years later, as Guyana celebrated its first fifty years of independence, Venezuela had cast that map aside – the map it celebrated in the name of Bolivar for over sixty years – to deny the new Guyana its own patrimony.

The Tri-Junction Point

It was not always so; in 1931, for example – and there are many such instances of Venezuelan official fidelity to the 1899 Award – in the context of the tri-junction point of the boundary between Brazil, Guyana and Venezuela, Venezuela insisted on staying strictly in accord with the 1899 Award and the Official Boundary Map. To a British proposal for a minor adjustment by agreement Venezuela argued that, for constitutional reasons, they would not depart from the letter of the 1899 Award. The Venezuelan Minister of Foreign Affairs, P. Itriago Chacín wrote (translation) on 31 October 1931 explaining their objection in principle to any change in the established border.

Venezuela rejects any change from the line of the 1899 Award

"At the present time also there exist objections of principle to an alteration by agreement to the frontier de droit, since, as this frontier is the result of a public treaty ratified by the Venezuelan legislature, it could only be modified by a process which would take considerable time even supposing that other difficulties, also of principle, could be got over."

As the Venezuelan Foreign Ministry had recorded assertively on 16 October 1931: *"This solution (*of rejected adjustment) *is the only one which allows of making the boundary one straight line between the sources of the Wenamo and Roraima,* **as required by the terms of the Award.** *"*

The entire exercise of marking the *tri-junction point* in 1931 was affirmative of the location of Guyana's boundary with Venezuela and of Venezuela's acknowledgement of it – on Mount Roraima, as determined by the 1899 Award. It was the starting point of marking Guyana's boundary with Brazil. Brazil borders Guyana and Venezuela: Guyana to the north; Venezuela to the north-west. The three boundaries meet at a point of intersection – the '*tri-junction*' point – the point where the boundaries converge and from which the boundary with Brazil would be marked. Venezuela was not involved in the course of the Guyana-Brazil boundary but was centrally involved in its commencement on the Guyana-Venezuela border. And, it was an exercise for Governments. The Guianese official, C.P. deFreitas, was appointed to the British Guiana Commission and in his memoir *On the Frontier* he explained how Venezuela's involvement worked:

On the Frontier, by C.P, deFreitas:

"It was decided that the two Commissions (for British Guiana and Brazil) would meet a Venezuelan Commission in the savannahs at the base of Mount Roraima, on the summit of which the boundaries of the three countries converge and meet. The three sections would then, as a mixed British-Brazilian-Venezuelan Commission decide on the location of this point and define and mark it. After this the Venezuelans would leave us and the British and Brazilian Commissions would, commencing from that point, start on the reconnaissance, surveys, definition and demarcation of the boundary between their two respective countries."

The tri-junction point on the plateau of Roraima was duly fixed and marked with a pyramid erected by the three Commissions. It was marked on its three faces pointing west, south and east: VENEZUELA. BRAZIL and BRITISH GUIANA respectively.

And the written records attest it:pp.48/9 of App.9 of UK Cmd. 6965 confirm as follows:

"Mark B/BG O at the Junction of BRITISH GUIANA, BRAZIL and VENEZUELA on Mount RORAIMA

"The pillar, on the side facing British Guiana, has a brass plate inscribed 'BRITISH GUIANA' in relief, and on the side facing Brazil, the arms of the Republic of Brazil, and below it "BRASIL – C.D.F.S.N. – 1931" outlined in quartz crystal. On the side facing Venezuela it has the Arms of the Republic of Venezuela and "VENEZUELA" outlined in quartz crystal."

The Tri-Junction Monument marking Venezuela's eastern border on Mt Roraima. (See page 52 re the plaque above)

Ten years later, into the early forties, a Venezuelan Foreign Minister, Dr Gil Borges, would reassure a British Ambassador in Caracas, D. St Clair Gainer, in the context of a press comment about the Arbitral Award, that – as the Ambassador reported him –

> *"From time to time an odd article about British Guiana appears in the Press but that I need take no notice of that; the articles were obviously written by persons of little knowledge who have never had access to official files. So far as the Venezuelan Government were concerned the one really satisfactory frontier Venezuela possessed (at that time) was the British Guiana frontier and it would not occur to them to dispute it."*

Ambassador Gainer was reassured that the matter was *'chose jugée'*, and said so to the Minister.

How much more worthy it would have been had Venezuela continued to adopt the candidly honest stand of its Foreign Minister as late as 1941. Sordid is the tale of how Venezuela abandoned the path of propriety, and with it the rule of law; and how, particularly now, its rulers seek to dispossess Guyana of its heritage and to mar the environment of our Region. It is a shameful imperial ambition.

Venezuelan greed revived

Guyana's controversies with Venezuela have always had a sharper edge than any other; perhaps because the former derive to a greater degree from cultivated avarice and calculated stratagems –all sustained by awareness of unequal strengths. These are not attributes of the Venezuelan people; they dwell within coteries of Venezuelan power, both civilian and military; and they are self-sustaining, feeding on their co-mingled myths and ambitions, and generating new falsehoods which they begin to believe.

For sixty years, Venezuelan Governments respected, adopted, even protected the 1899 boundary; yet today President Maduro can say in a studied distortion of history: *With the 20th century came the third stage. The Treaty of Paris was denounced as invalid.* By 'the Treaty of Paris' he means the Arbitral Tribunal that met in Paris and the Award of 1899 and the demarcated boundary that Venezuela respected for sixty years of that 20th century – another distortion on which is being built another stratagem of dispossession: one that may have as much, or little, to do with Venezuela's internal political maelstrom as Guyana-Venezuela relations.

In 2016, as Guyana looked to marking with pride the 50th Anniversary of its Independence, the settlement of its border with Venezuela – secured by the 1899 Arbitral Award and its formal demarcation – that settlement was brusquely threatened by forces in Caracas – in furtherance of their earlier efforts to subvert the rules of international law and virtually steal Guyana's substance.

Satisfied initially with its achievements under the 1899 Award, though not without the grumbles of the greedy who wanted even more, Venezuela proceeded toward fulfilment of the destiny which the vast mineral wealth its land yielded – including from the Orinoco Basin that the Award gave them; and without which that region would still be in contention. Through most of the first half of the 20th century, as has been shown, official Venezuela found no quarrel with the Award; and when in 1962 it chose to reopen it with Britain – some sixty years after it had insistently closed it – it did so with restraint and circumspection in the manner of equals. But time was on the side of those in Venezuela for whom, with national wealth now assured, eastward expansion had become an imperial crusade. And the ground was well prepared.

The Mallet-Prevost stratagem

At the first sign of Guyana's movement to independence, the Venezuelan Government initiated a vigorous boundary controversy on the most tenuous of grounds. The single source of these grounds was, and remains to this day, a memorandum written by an American lawyer, Severo Mallet-Prevost, who was one of the junior counsel for Venezuela during the Arbitral Tribunal's hearing. It was written in 1944 just after he had received from the Government of Venezuela the Order of the Liberator for his services to the Republic. But the slanderous tale was not told then. It was embedded in a secret memorandum dictated to his law partner in Washington in 1944 with strict instructions that it be opened and published only after his death. He died in 1949 – when every other participant in the arbitral proceedings had themselves long since died.

The posthumous memorandum contended by conjecture ('I became convinced and still believe") that the Arbitral Award of 1899 was the result of a political deal between Britain and Russia carried into effect by collusion between the British Judges and the Russian President of the Tribunal and agreed to in the interest of unanimity by the American Judges – after they had consulted with the American lawyers (including himself) who were Venezuela's chosen counsel. How callous a conjecture!

Yet, it was on this flimsiest pretext of an old and disappointed man's posthumous memoirs set down some 45 years after the events – these shreds and patches embroidered with speculations, ambiguities and allusions to new but undisclosed evidence, these calumnies against five of the most eminent jurists in the world of their time – that Venezuela mounted its international campaign against Guyana as it approached independence.

After Dr Jagan had raised the issue of Guyana's Independence in the United Nations in late 1961 and spoke in the Fourth Committee on 18 December 1961, Venezuela for the first time questioned in that organisation their border with then British Guiana. It did so in February 1962 in the Fourth Committee, but was at pains to emphasise its innocence – as in the conversation of the Minister Counsellor of the Venezuelan Mission to the UN, Walter Brandt, which the US Mission recorded on 15 January 1962 referring to an Aide Memoire of 12 January 1962; both records now declassified.

Extract from the US State Department's Memorandum of Conversation dated 15 January 1962 with Mr Walter Brandt of the Venezuelan Permanent Mission to the UN

"He explained that Venezuela was not questioning the legality of the Arbitral Award but felt it only just that the Award should be revised since it was handed down by a Tribunal of five judges which did not include on it any Venezuelans; .... Venezuela considers the Award to have been inequitable and questionable from a moral point of view (viciado).

"Mr Brandt indicated that Venezuela's contemplated action in the Fourth Committee was not intended to be construed as a Venezuelan request to re-open the boundary question, nor was it an attempt to block any possible UN gesture in favour of British Guiana's independence."

Of course, as events were to confirm, these contentions of innocence were soon abandoned. The Arbitral Award became not 'immoral' but 'null and void'; and no 'block' on British Guiana's Independence became insistence that it should not happen unless the border was revised. As the date for Independence drew nearer the agitation grew fiercer threatening in veiled and indirect ways the advance to Independence itself. Hence the British conversations in Geneva in 1966 – three months before Guyana's Independence.

The 'Cold War' dimension

But there was more, until now, hidden in archival secrecy. Though long suspected, American State Papers (both White House and State Department Papers since declassified) have now revealed a darker plot. In the 1950s and 1960s, in a 'cold war' context, there was serious Western concern, mainly driven by the United States, that Guyana's independence under a Jagan-led Government would see another Cuba, this time on the South American Continent. In 1962, the then Venezuelan President, Rómulo Betancourt, chose to take advantage of this fear of 'another Cuba' in an independent Guyana by proposing a plan to develop the Essequibo region by US and British investors no longer as part of British Guiana – but under 'Venezuelan sovereignty' – a pretext for intervention and acquisition under the guise of curbing the spread of' 'communism'.

A despatch of 15 May 1962 from the American Ambassador in Caracas (C. Allan Stewart) conveyed to the State Department Betancourt's views on the "border question" as gleaned "during the course of several meetings" with him. He wrote with the astuteness of a seasoned diplomat:

> *"President Betancourt professes to be greatly concerned about an independent British Guiana with Cheddie Jagan as Prime Minister. He suspects that Jagan is already too committed to communism and that his American wife exercises considerable influence over him... This alarm may be slightly simulated since Betancourt's solution of the border dispute presupposes a hostile Jagan.*

> *"His plan: Through a series of conferences with the British before Guiana is awarded independence a cordon sanitaire would be set up between the present boundary line and one*

mutually agreed upon by the two countries (Venezuela and Britain). Sovereignty of this slice of British Guiana would pass to Venezuela. ...

"Of course, the reason for the existence of the strip of territory, according to the President, is the danger of communist infiltration of Venezuela from British Guiana if a Castro-type government ever were established... It would seem logical that Venezuela will from now on pursue the idea of the cordon sanitaire to protect itself from a commie-line independent British Guiana rather than send support to the Burnham opposition."

A year later, on 30 June 1963, President Kennedy was meeting Britain's Prime Minister Macmillan at Birch Grove in England and, on the American side, the issue of British Guiana was the *"principal subject the President intend(ed) to raise with Macmillan"*. So wrote Dean Rusk (the American Secretary of State) the week before in a secret telegram to Ambassador Bruce (the U.S. Ambassador in London) seeking his thoughts *"on how best to convince our British friends of the deadly seriousness of our concern and our determination that British Guiana shall not become independent with a Communist government."* The commonality of motivation between Kennedy and Betancourt was quite remarkable. Much more remarkable is the inheritance, adoption and vigorous pursuit of an abandoned CIA legacy by an avowed, radical, anti-imperialist Venezuelan Government of the present – and in the name of Bolivar.

Of course, none of this was ever revealed to the Venezuelan people whose patriotism was infused with the simplistic fallacy that Venezuela was 'robbed' by Britain of the Essequibo region of Guyana. On their maps, and in their minds, it was the *'Zona en Reclamacion'*. As it transpired, it was Jagan's political opponent,

Burnham, who led the Independent Guyana. But by then, driven by Venezuela's greed, the 'controversy' had taken on a life of its own, certainly for the chauvinistic forces that had nurtured it. For those forces the Mallet-Prevost fable would suffice to perpetuate the contention that the 1899 Arbitral Award is 'null and void' and the Essequibo region automatically Venezuelan, studiously ignoring the implications of the nullity contention for their own Orinoco Delta which the same Award had given to them. That was and is today Venezuela's basic contention – that the 1899 Arbitral Award is 'null and void' because of the Mallet-Prevost posthumous memoire.

The 'David and Goliath' torment

The young, and powerless, Guyana faced this 'David and Goliath' situation, and its attendant harassment, from birth. Its only defence was diplomacy: an appeal to the international community to save the infant state from the machinations of its large, wealthy, powerful – and alas, unscrupulous – neighbour. And in those days, Venezuela pursued its territorial ambitions shamelessly. Guyana was kept out of the Organisation of American States (OAS) until 1991 and, within months of independence, it brazenly breached the border (on Ankoko Island) in defiance of the Geneva Agreement. The same year it began interfering in Guyana's internal affairs through attempted subversion of Guyana's indigenous people. In 1968, as Guyana's Prime Minister paid an official visit to Britain, Venezuela unashamedly bought advertising space in the London *Times* (of 15 June), announcing its non-recognition of concessions granted by Guyana in the area it 'claimed'. Later that year, contemptuous of international law, President Leoni issued a 'decree' purporting to annex a strip of territorial waters adjacent to Guyana's coast. It refused, of course, to sign the Law of the Sea Convention – one of the few countries in the world to exclude itself from '*the Constitution for the Oceans*'. The young Guyana faced fearful odds. Surmounting them became Guyana's mission in the world.

In the General Debate of the 23rd session of the United Nations General Assembly (on 3 October 1968), Guyana devoted its entire Address to the issue of Venezuela's attempts to stifle Guyana at birth. It was called; *Development or Defence: the Small State threatened with Aggression.* It was to continue to be an apt description of Guyana's predicament throughout the ensuing years.

It has been earlier indicated how, in rejecting Venezuela's devious attempts to defer Guyana's Independence, Britain sought to rid the new Guyana of the Venezuelan 'plague'. February 17th, 2016 was the 50th anniversary of the signing of the 1966 Geneva Agreement. It is not co-incidental that 2016 was also the 50th Anniversary of Guyana's Independence; for the Geneva Meeting represented the last effort from Caracas to prevent Guyana's Independence.

The Geneva Agreement, 1966

The Geneva Agreement was between Britain and Venezuela; Guyana only became a party on attaining Independence. And that is what it was essentially about – Guyana's Independence. Until then, Venezuela had indulged an argument with Britain that Bolivar's legacy could never have blessed, namely, to retain the status of colonialism in British Guiana until the boundary with Venezuela was changed. The Geneva Agreement ended that un-Bolivarian argument. Guyana would be free with its borders intact. That is why Guyana believed the Geneva Agreement was worth commemorating; and it said so. It is part of the founding instruments of Guyana's freedom.

In that context, the Agreement carefully identified the nature of Venezuela's on-going controversy with Britain as "the controversy between Venezuela and the United Kingdom which has arisen as a result of the Venezuelan contention that the arbitral award of 1899 about the frontier between British Guiana and Venezuela is null and void." It was with this controversy' that the Geneva "conversations", and their outcome in the form of the Geneva Agreement, was concerned. Having identified the controversy as that raised by Venezuela's contention of nullity of the 1899 Arbitral Award, the Geneva Agreement went on to stipulate the means which the Parties agreed must be followed to resolve that controversy.

The Agreement provided a clear path to settlement ending in judicial process. First, there would be a four-year Mixed Commission of Guyanese and Venezuelan representatives, and if the Commission could not settle the matter and the Governments could not agree on the next means of doing so, the United Nations Secretary-General would be the arbiter of the "means of settlement" from those set out in Article 33 of the Charter of the United Nations. U Thant was the UN Secretary-General in 1966 and on receipt of the Agreement he replied on 4 April 1966 without equivocation.

United Nations Secretary-General's acceptance of obligations under the Geneva Agreement

H.E. U Thant, 4 April 1966 to the Foreign Minister of Venezuela –

"I have made note of the obligations that eventually can fall on the Secretary-General of the United Nations by virtue of Paragraph 2 of Article IV of the Agreement and it pleases me to inform you that the functions are of such a nature that they can be appropriately carried out by the Secretary-General of the United Nations."

The Mixed Commission did not succeed in resolving the controversy. Guyana's Representatives were Sir Donald Jackson (a former Chief Justice of British Guiana) and Dr Mohammed Shahabuddeen (later, a Judge of the ICJ). The Commission held many meetings during their four-year existence. At the very first meeting Guyana invited

Venezuela to produce its evidence and arguments in support of its claim that the Arbitral Award was 'null and void'. Venezuela's response was that the issue of 'nullity' was not an issue with which the Mixed Commission should concern itself. The only issue before the Mixed Commission was how much of the Essequibo region was Guyana prepared to cede either directly or within the framework of a 'Joint Development' programme. The minutes of the Meetings of the Mixed Commission were carefully recorded and signed with copies attached to the Final Report and Interim Reports were issued to both Governments signed by the Commissioners.

In declining to address their basic legal contention of nullity in the Mixed Commission, the Venezuelan Commissioners did, however, concede that the question of judicial settlement could arise at a later time.: *'The juridical examination of the question* (of nullity) *would, if necessary, be proceeded with, in time, by some international tribunal in accordance with article IV of the Geneva Agreement'*. So said Venezuela at the end of 1966 – in the First Interim Report signed in Caracas by the Venezuelan Commissioners Luis Loreto and G Garcia Bustillos. Today, fifty-five years on, Venezuela still argues that that later 'time' has not yet come.

Fifty years of Venezuelan 'filibuster'

The Mixed Commission's failure to find a resolution to the controversy was due as much to what was said in the Commission as to what was done by Venezuela beyond the discussions. There has been allusion to some of them above, namely, Venezuela's:

- Violation of Guyana's territorial integrity on Ankoko Island
- The Leoni attempt to appropriate Guyana's off-shore waters
- Economic aggression through campaigns against investment in Guyana
- Intervention in Guyana's internal affairs through the Rupununi 'uprising'.

And there were others. What the experience of the Mixed Commission revealed was a strategy which Venezuela has pursued for over fifty years, namely: a façade of peaceful but fruitless discussion masking a policy of studied political, economic and increasingly militaristic aggression. When the Geneva meeting was held in 1966, the expectation was a process of some ten years to solution. Under the Protocol of Port of Spain, a moratorium of twelve years followed the Mixed Commission, with similar periods of renewal as a guarantee of peaceable neighbourly relations. But Venezuela found it too cramping of its strategy and refused to extend the moratorium. Then followed twenty-seven years of a UN 'good offices' process which yielded nothing by way of solution but suited Venezuela's strategy of filibustered belligerence. With the untimely death of the last Personal Representative of the Secretary-General under that process, the much respected Dr Norman Girvan, Guyana in September 2014 communicated to the Secretary-General of the United Nations its firm view that the process had run its course.

Yet Venezuela ensures that it remains a matter of contention, though not surprisingly (given President Betancourt's' manoeuvres) less rancorous in the time of Hugo Chavez than in earlier years. However, beyond Chavez, his successor President Nicolás Maduro, whatever the internal political influences, has carried Venezuela's campaign of usurpation to even more outrageous lengths – threatening both the maritime and territorial integrity of Guyana – and reaching beyond Guyana, to the maritime space of other Caribbean Community countries. And abandoning every vestige of civility.

Destroying International Agreements

A former Foreign Minister of a Central American country once described successive Governments of his neighbouring country as "serial killers of international agreements". It was an apt description. It could not be bettered as a description of Venezuela in its relations with Guyana: *SERIAL KILLERS OF INTERNATIONAL*

AGREEMENTS: the charge is a serious one; it should not be advanced without good reason and irrefutable evidence; for its proof proclaims the lowest rank of internationalism and shameful conduct in a time when the world has set high standards of civilized behaviour for nations no less than people. But it is a charge that Venezuela invites -with good reason and irrefutable evidence.

Let a start be made with the Treaty of Munster of 1648. The middle of the 17th century was a long time ago. Venezuela as a State was yet to be born. European powers were contending for space in South America. The Treaty of Munster between Spain and the Netherlands was essentially about their occupancies; and in particular about the assured place of the Dutch in the region that would be Brazil, Venezuela and the Guianas. From the Essequibo to the Orinoco, watched over by Kyk Over Al, from the Atlantic through the Pomeroon region, the Treaty of Munster laid out Guyana's Dutch beginnings. As Justice Brewer suggested in the 1899 Arbitral proceedings [vol. 8 p. 2234, etc]:

> *"the Spanish authorities recognized that the concession, or confirmation, or whatever you call it, in the Treaty, was not that simply the island of Kijkoveral, but of territory appurtenant thereto and considered that the Pomeroon was really appurtenant to the Essequibo..."*

and, later [in vol.9 at p.2648-9],

> *"whether we are to look upon them in that attitude or whether we should look upon them then as coming into vacant territory, nobody being in Kijkoveral, nobody being in the Essequibo, and occupying possessions and territory not then occupied, and therefore entitled not to the mere area on which it rests, but to all the fringe, as my Lord Justice Collins happily expressed it and all the surroundings which become appurtenant to that occupation."*

But that did not suit Venezuelan ambition and so the Treaty had to be transfigured – this interpretation had to be killed. So, according to Venezuela, the Treaty of Munster – with which they had nothing to do – must be understood, 250 years later, to mean that Spain ceded to the Dutch only the places they actually possessed by then in Guiana, and that what was not ceded was retained by Spain. The British argument was that Holland did not derive title by cession, and was not so limited; that the Treaty did not give any paramount effect to Spain's alleged title by discovery and that Holland was at liberty to expand her possessions into areas of Guiana not actually held and possessed by Spain at the date of the Treaty.

The British argument was one more in accord with the actual language of the Treaty and was one that the Tribunal clearly adopted.- as had the United States Commission that preceded it – and of which Justice Brewer was Chairman. It is a view that accorded with the views afterwards expressed by Huber in his authoritative and closely reasoned award in the *Island of Palmas* Case – where he said that the Treaty of Munster prescribed no frontiers and appointed no definite regions as belonging to one power or the other, but established as a criterion "the principle of possession". He also took the view that the Treaty indirectly refused to recognize the title based on discovery.

These arguments are not for review as in the nature of an appeal; but Venezuela understood that they had to be killed off in support of a historical argument assuming success for their concocted argument that the Award of the Tribunal is 'null and void'. Their first act of assassination of the relevant international agreements was the hallowed Treaty of Munster of 1648 – first targeted during the hearing of the Court of Arbitration of 1899.

They did quite well in the Arbitration: in the words of their lawyers "securing to Venezuela the mouth of the Orinoco and control of the Orinoco Basin, these being the most important questions at issue."

And, as we have seen, for sixty years afterwards they adopted, respected – even protected – the boundary as awarded by the Tribunal and demarcated on the ground: all under the Treaty of Washington of 1897, which they concluded with Britain and ratified by their Congress.

But there came a time when the forces of greed became ascendant in Venezuela and they had to find ways to abandon their satisfaction with the boundary. They turned to many devices: posthumous memoirs, even 'cold war' artifices. But the biggest impediment of all was the Treaty of Washington itself under which the Arbitration Tribunal was set up, the Award made, and the Boundary established. For the covetous forces in Venezuela the answer was clear – the Treaty of Washington had to go. Another assassination of an age old Treaty.

The most recent description of the killing of this venerable international agreement which had brought peace and calm and good neighbourliness to the frontier of Guyana and Venezuela for over sixty years was given on 28 March 2016. The words are those of President Maduro himself in a studied and much publicized interview to teleSUR:

> *"The plundering of Venezuela, as I have described, was carried out via a flawed treaty, which Venezuela considers invalid and does not recognize."*

Not all Venezuelans, assuredly, will interpret history thus; but President Maduro speaks for the Government of Venezuela. As such, he seems to have forgotten that Venezuela's title to the Orinoco basin about which his lawyers were so pleased in 1899, derives from that 'flawed treaty' and the Award of the Tribunal under it. Guyana has not forgotten.

But not all crimes follow the same path. Unlike the Treaty of Washington which is declared invalid and no longer recognized by

Venezuela, the Geneva Agreement, 1966 is recognized but distorted. A distortion of its intent and meaning is fundamental to Venezuela's strategy for stealing from its young neighbour more than a half of its land. The Geneva Agreement, which ended Venezuela's desperate effort to forestall Guyana's Independence with its borders intact, set out a clear path for bringing finality to Venezuela's basic contention that the Arbitral Award of 1899 is 'null and void'.

The Sanctity of Treaties

Nothing can be clearer from the text of the Agreement and its history that this is the issue for which the Agreement provides a path of settlement through the authority it entrusts to the United Nations Secretary-General – a path which could lead to a definitive settlement by judicial process. But Venezuela's conduct is in violation of the rule of international law and the last thing it wants is the application of law to its lawless behaviour. So, they must distort the Agreement to ignore the contention of 'nullity' and go back to the Treaty of Munster of 1648, and indeed, before that to a Papal Bull of the fifteenth century, or better still – since (in Venezuelan eyes) the Treaty of Munster is really gone and the Treaty of Washington is invalid – pursue a strategy of continuous but fruitless discussion as a cover for constant harassment of a weak neighbour. So the real Geneva Agreement is disposed of and a falsified one celebrated.

Despite Venezuela's efforts, the Treaty of Munster retains its ancient meaning, the Treaty of Washington continues to sustain all that has been done in its name and the Geneva Agreement in its true meaning subsists to secure the definitive settlement of the controversy of nullity that plagues Guyana-Venezuela relations. Being a serial killer of international agreements is often, therefore, a matter of intent, and injurious to the party against whom directed only if allowed to be. But there could be a wider impact. At stake, if such conduct is not denounced, is the sanctity of treaties at a global level.

International comity rests on the preservation of such sanctity; and every effort to dethrone it anywhere hurts the international community everywhere. Venezuela's efforts to destroy international agreements in its relations with Guyana, inflicts a global wound and calls for global condemnation.

Venezuela describes itself as the Bolivarian Republic of Venezuela. Simon Bolivar is a great hero of the Hemisphere whose name is a symbol of freedom from colonialism, Spanish colonialism specially. Yet it is in the name of Spanish colonialism that Venezuela seeks to hoist its flag over Guyana's Essequibo region – more than half of Guyana. It was to become a voracious craving of Venezuela – already nearly 4 ½ times the size of Guyana; with a population of 28.8 million, almost 3,600 per cent more than Guyana.

With these gross *David and Goliath* disparities Venezuela's crusade is being driven now by a regime that presents itself as the Hemisphere's anti-imperialist champion. The Maduro regime is a contradiction in terms. In its reliance on propaganda and demagoguery it has abandoned even a semblance of argument. For sixty years Venezuela cherished the 1899 Award; now President Maduro discards even the need to explain that away and resorts to bluster and flagrant falsehoods.

Rogue States

How can that happen in a world in which relations between nations are governed by acceptable universal norms and the rule of law is supposed to prevail – in a world in which all countries are pledged to respect and uphold the principles and purposes of the Charter of the United Nations? The answer is that States which consistently flout international law are 'rogue states'; and this is a title which Venezuela should be careful to avoid. It is in this sense that Guyana calls upon Venezuela to change course and to abide by the rule of law.

What Venezuela describes as its 'claim' to Essequibo is rooted, as shown, in its rejection of every relevant international agreement over five centuries – from the Treaty of Munster in 1648, to the Treaty of Washington in 1897, to the Geneva Agreement in 1966. Is it any wonder that the place Venezuela least wants to go is the International Court of Justice? They are afraid of internationalism, they are afraid of judicial process, they are afraid of what justice will require of them.

It follows that the cause is not only Guyana's. Were Venezuela's stratagems to prevail, the frontiers of innumerable countries the world over would be in jeopardy; for the sanctity of treaties which is the glue holding the international community of states together, would have melted. Guyana's resistance of Venezuela's perverse contentions is a global service.

The Venezuelan claim of a massive chunk of Guyana's territory is a calumny born of greed, nurtured by falsity and fable, and maintained by political demagoguery. It is a claim that is contemptuous of the rule of international law and scornful of the sanctity of treaties. It is a claim that threatens the sovereignty and territorial integrity of Guyana and the peace of its region of the world. The 55th year of Guyana's Independence cries out for release from this iniquity.

Part II

A clear path to judicial settlement

On 2nd December 2014, the Minister of Foreign Affairs of Guyana, Carolyn Rodrigues-Birkett wrote her counterpart in Caracas observing that, after 25 years, the 'good offices' process had not brought the Parties any closer to a resolution of the controversy. She stated that her Government was *"reviewing the other options under Article 33 of the United Nations Charter, as provided for by the 1966 Geneva Agreement, that could serve to bring to an end the controversy"*. In September 2015, Guyana's new President, David Granger, called upon the Secretary-General of the United Nations, Ban Ki-moon, to have Venezuela's contention that the Arbitral Award of 1899 is 'null and void' settled with finality by judicial process under the Geneva Agreement

President Granger's Address to the UN General Assembly, 29th September 2015

"From the beginning of Guyana's independence ... Venezuela has resorted to various stratagems to deprive us of our territory. ...We thank the United Nations and the Secretary-General for appointing various officials during the past 25 years to use their good offices to help to resolve this controversy. We feel, however, that the process has now been exhausted, Guyana does not want this obnoxious territorial

claim to obscure our country's prospects for peace and obstruct its potential growth for the next 50 years. We need a permanent solution if we are to avoid a fate of perpetual peril and penury, and we seek a judicial settlement to the controversy... The United Nations remains our best hope and prospect for peace, the best assurance of security for small States."

Venezuela continued to pressure the Secretary-General *"to commence the process of appointing a Good Officer"* succeeding Dr Girvan.

S.G. Ban Ki-moon's 'Way Forward'

As repository of the duty to choose a means of settlement, Secretary-General Ban Ki-moon retained a 'good office' process with a 'way forward' route-map ending with a possible referral of the controversy to the International Court of Justice – in the absence of settlement by the end of 2016. He decided, however, that before he left office, he would give 'good offices', with a strengthened element of mediation, a last chance in 2017. To that end, after consultation with his successor, S.G. Antonio Guterres, he decided that there would be a 'final' year, terminating at the end of 2017, when a settlement would be sought through the efforts of a personal representative of S.G. Guterres. S.G. Ban Ki-moon's decision of 15th December 2016 was unequivocal:

"if by the end of 2017, the Secretary-General concludes that significant progress has not been made toward arriving at a full agreement for the solution of the controversy, he will choose the International Court of Justice as the next means of settlement"

In S.G. Ban Ki-moon's decision letter of 15 December 2016 he defined the 'controversy' with clarity, namely. that "which has arisen as a result of the Venezuelan contention that the Arbitral Award of 1899 about the frontier between British Guiana and Venezuela is null and void'. So, as well, did the first paragraph of the Terms of Reference of the Secretary-General's Personal Representative.

Even before 2016 ended, the Secretary-General received a response to his 15 December 'decision letter' from the Government of Guyana, and more personally from Guyana's President, David Granger, who wrote:

> *Secretary-General, I convey to you Guyana's full acceptance of the decision, and our determination to do all in our power to fulfil its objectives. We accept your good offices proposal for a final period of twelve months and that, if by the end of 2017 the Secretary-General concludes that there has not been "significant progress" on a full agreement for the solution of the controversy, the Secretary-General will choose the International Court of Justice as the next means of settlement under the Geneva Agreement.*

The President wrote likewise to President Maduro to extend a hand of friendship and to assure him of Guyana's readiness to cooperate in the areas the Secretary-General had indicated and, more generally, in the time-bound good offices process.

Four Secretaries-General

As the Guyana -Venezuela controversy reached Secretary-General Guterres at the end of 2017, it had come on the desk of four UN Secretaries-General: S.G. U Thant, S.G. Perez de Cuellar, S.G. Ban Ki-moon and S.G. Antonio Guterres – over a period of 51 years; and at no time in those years had the controversy been more tempestuous and more of a threat to peace than it was then.

Guyana's Full Cooperation

On 5 January, 2017 Guyana's President Granger welcomed Secretary-General Guterres to his new office, recalled S.G. Ban Ki-moon's letter of 15 December 2016 and assured him of the Government of Guyana's commitment to its objectives "in respect of both the coming twelve (12) month 'good offices' process and any recourse to the International Court of Justice that may be necessary thereafter."

Guyana used the first days of 2017 in preparing for the Personal Representative to be appointed by S.G. Guterres, an introductory memorandum on the Guyana-Venezuela controversy intended to be of assistance to the Personal Representative. This, with its annexures, was presented to Dag Nylander as early as possible after notification of his appointment by the S.G.'s letter of 23 February 2017. The first paragraph made clear Guyana's assumption that the new process *"begins on 1 January 2017 and continues until 31 December 2017."*

The Personal Representative, as required by his Terms of Reference, reported to the Secretary-General twice formally before his final November report. Exchanges in the process were agreed to be 'confidential' ; so it is not the purpose here to traverse the trodden ground; but to call attention to some aspects of the journey in 2017 pertinent to the question whether or not 'significant progress' had or had not been made during the year toward arriving at a full agreement for the solution of the controversy between Guyana and Venezuela, which has arisen as a result of the Venezuelan contention that the Arbitral Award of 1899 between British Guiana and Venezuela is null and void.

If, as a matter of fact, such 'significant progress' was not made, the Secretary- General would so conclude, and would choose the International Court of Justice as the next means of settlement. Progress, or its absence, would be evident.

Venezuelan Militarism Paramount

At the half way point in 2017, (24 June), a ceremonial military parade in Caracas (commemorating the Battle of Carabobo) was dominated by the orchestrated chant: *"el sol de Venezuela nace en el Essequibo"* – *"the Venezuelan sun rises in the Essequibo"* – answered by the Commander in Chief, President Maduro himself – *"nace en el Essequibo"*: a Venezuelan war cry in the middle of the U.N.'s confabulation of peace.

This does not answer directly the question of 'progress' from dialogue: but it gives an indication of the mood toward progress in the government of Venezuela at a critical point in the process. It was to continue to the end – inflammatory sloganeering urged on Venezuela's military while the Secretary-General's Personal Representative was urging peaceful resolution.

Venezuela rejects 'Confidence Building'

The Personal Representative's Terms of Reference attached paramountcy to early progress on 'Confidence Building Measures' – measures to improve the environment for dialogue. Guyana (led by its Foreign Minister, Carl Greenidge) worked hard at reviving earlier efforts at bilateral cooperation in fisheries, in border security and in forestry; and advanced structured proposals for starting with forestry. Venezuela was not interested in CBMs; and that wing of the PR's mandate collapsed.

Bilateral Meetings Falter

The process never got to 'the controversy' until 28 October 2017. Then followed three Bilateral Meetings organised by the S.G.'s Personal Representative – at *'Greentree'*, a well-established 'retreat' outside New York for quiet inter-locution. Whatever the PR's expectations, there was no 'progress'; much less 'significant progress' at *Greentree*. As Guyana reflected on the occasion, not only was no progress made, but Venezuela showed how far from the potential for 'progress' their current adversarial mood had carried them.

As the *Greentree* Bilaterals ended with implausible intimations of hope from Venezuela, their President was already at work in adversarial manner giving form to Venezuela's territorial claim. On 2nd November 2017, Venezuela officially reported President Maduro as proclaiming Venezuela's ascent of Mt Roraima (the border mountain shared with Guyana and Brazil), defacing in the process the 'BRITISH GUIANA' plaque on the Tri-Junction Monument erected jointly in 1931, as earlier described. The charade of course could not erase the Boundary reality that the monument itself marked. The farce was to proclaim Guyana's Essequibo Region beyond the tri-point as being within the Venezuelan horizon. It was a threat and warning of physical occupation ahead. Guyana immediately sent a Note of Protest to Caracas, and a copy to the S.G.'s Personal Representative. As late as the month of the PR's Final Report to the Secretary-General, Venezuela was defying in bombastic manner, the UN's call for peaceful settlement.

The Meaning of 'Significant Progress'

In answering whether 'significant progress' had been made in 2017 every word of the Secretary-General's careful formulation was meaningful: 'toward arriving at a full agreement': not 'a partial agreement', nor a 'temporary agreement'; not a 'fractional' agreement, nor a 'limited' agreement; but a 'full' agreement – an all-encompassing agreement; an agreement that puts the controversy to rest. The 2017 process had not even hinted at such an agreement, much less made progress toward it. An 'agreement' 'for a solution': the bar is high. Not a promise of light, but dawn itself; there was not even a lifting of the darkness. And a 'solution' to what? Not just to unfriendly relations, or quarrels over hostile behaviour. No; solution to a specific controversy between Guyana and Venezuela; the controversy, as the Secretary-General had particularised it: *"which has arisen as a result of the Venezuelan contention that the Arbitral Award of 1899 about the frontier between British Guiana and Venezuela is null and void."*

The 2017 process never got close to discussing this controversy until the month before the PR's Final Report – despite Guyana's (and the PR's) early and repeated efforts to engage this 'core issue': Venezuela's contention of nullity of the Arbitral Award – its essential, indispensable, basic, cardinal contention. They refused that long to engage it.

It was as if having raised the 'contention' – however illegitimate and absurd -Venezuela believes that a 'controversy' has arisen which Guyana has a duty to help to resolve – regardless of the contention itself. It might be absurd, irrational, incongruous, even bizarre; but this is the way power speaks to the powerless, the strong to the weak, the rich to the poor: *you must surrender, justice regardless, because my might demands it.* The rule of strong men; not the rule of law – everything which the United Nations – its purposes and its principles – stands against. And worst of all Venezuela's absurdities: we will use the machinery of the United Nations itself to get our lawless way – starting in the Committee on Decolonisation – of all places: truncating, if it can, Guyana's unquestionable right of self-determination.

"Moving Forward"

Two other observations are pertinent. In the penultimate paragraph of the Terms of Reference from Secretary-General Guterres to his Personal Representative he specifically directed that in his third and final Report, in the context of 'moving forward' *"the mediator will take into account the decision of the Secretary-General communicated to the parties on 15 December 2016, that he will choose the International Court of Justice as the next means of settlement of the controversy if significant progress is not achieved by the end of 2017."* Not only did this direction reiterate the Secretary-General's commitment, it reminded the Personal Representative that failure to make progress in the process ending 2017 was not a total failure; since there would follow as the next means of settlement – the International Court of Justice. This was the intent of the Geneva Agreement – a resolution of the controversy, if necessary, in the last resort, by judicial settlement. There is no need to search for other processes. This is the explicit decision of the two Secretaries-General to whom that decision fell; and their clear direction that it be followed.

The other observation relevant to 'moving forward' is the nature of the controversy. Secretary-General Ban Ki-moon put it best in his first meeting with President Granger when, talking about the controversy, he reflected: "It's a legal issue; it needs a legal answer". It was not a studied official response to the problem; but it was a wise one. Venezuela's challenge to the validity of an Award of a Court of Arbitration established under an international Treaty is a legal challenge. Its contention of nullity – of the Arbitral Award being 'null and void' – is a legal contention. For over 50 years Venezuela had side-stepped the legal issue it had opened up. In moving forward, it was now to the Court that settles such issues under international law that the Parties ought to go. By the Geneva Agreement, Britain and Venezuela agreed that one day the 'controversy' may go there for resolution. That day had come.

At the end of 2017, the course from Secretary-General U Thant to Secretary-General Antonio Guterres had been run. It was an unassailable fact that in 2017 there had been no progress, much less no 'significant' progress, toward arriving at an agreement; even less a 'full' agreement for a solution to the controversy between Guyana and Venezuela which has arisen as a result of the Venezuelan contention that the Arbitral Award of 1899 about the frontier between (what is now) Guyana and Venezuela – is null and void. International law and its just practice had now to take its course, with the United Nations faithful to its mandate of peace and justice and its specific commitment to observing it. Dialogue had been allowed to run its full course. The alternative to going to the ICJ in a timely manner was the military escalation of this controversy of which Venezuela had given unmistakable warning.

The Secretary-General 'chooses'

On 30th January 2018 – almost 52 years of Venezuela trying and failing to nullify the Paris outcome – the Secretary-General of the United Nations, Antonio Guterres, indicated to the Presidents of Guyana and Venezuela that:

> "I have fulfilled the responsibility that has fallen to me within the framework set by my predecessor and, significant progress not having been made toward arriving at a full agreement for the solution of the controversy, I have chosen the International Court of Justice as the means that is now to be used for its solution".
>
> **U.N. Secretary-General, Antonio Guterres, 30.1.2018**

By the Geneva Agreement both Venezuela and Guyana had agreed to follow the procedure chosen by the Secretary-General. Both had consented to the Court's jurisdiction if that was the means of settlement he determined should be pursued.

On 29th March 2018, Guyana filed in the Registry of the International Court of Justice an Application with regard to a dispute concerning **"the legal validity and binding effect of the Award regarding the Boundary between the Colony of British Guiana and the United States of Venezuela of 3 October 1899."** Venezuela, however, demurred. In a letter to the President of the Court of 18th June 2018 the President of Venezuela, Nicholas Maduro, conveyed that *"Venezuela will not participate in the proceedings that the Cooperative Republic of Guyana intends to initiate through a unilateral action."*

The letter itself stated that Venezuela had *'never accepted the jurisdiction of the Court ... due to its historical and fundamental institutions (and still less) would it accept the unilateral presentation of the request made by Guyana nor the form and content of the claims expressed therein"*. It asserted that *"there exists no basis that could establish… the Court's jurisdiction to consider Guyana's claims."* The ICJ duly decided that, in the circumstances of the case, it was necessary first of all to resolve the question of its jurisdiction, and that this question should accordingly be separately determined before any proceedings on the merits. This the Court did at a 'virtual' Oral Hearing on 30 June 2020.

Oral Hearing on 30 June 2020

The Court had fixed time limits for the filing of the Memorial on Jurisdiction by Guyana and the Counter-Memorial on Jurisdiction by Venezuela. Venezuela failed to submit its Counter-Memorial on Jurisdiction by the date fixed by the Court (April 18, 2019); but promised *information in order to assist the Court*. Then, on the deadline imposed by the Court for the receipt of such 'information' – 28 November 2019 – Venezuela submitted what it described as a 'Memorandum' (including its Annex) through which it sought to influence the proceedings, without participating properly in them.

The Hearing on 30th June 2020 was strictly about the Court's jurisdiction. Article 36(6) of the ICJ's Statute provides that "in the event of a dispute as to whether the Court has jurisdiction, the matter shall be settled by the decision of the Court'. Guyana argued that the technical requirements for that jurisdiction, like the consent of

Venezuela, were fully met. But, beyond technical argument, to the people of Guyana, the Court's authority rested as well on the central purpose of the Court itself – to render justice 'in all matters provided for in the Charter of the United Nations or in treaties or conventions in force'.

The Court's Jurisdiction

Basically, Venezuela was seeking to deny the Court jurisdiction to uphold the sanctity of treaties. Upholding the Vienna Convention on the Law of Treaties (in large measure a codification of international customary law) is unquestionably a 'purpose' of the Court. The Convention's avowal that *'Treaties must be observed in good faith' (art. 26)* is an element of this Court's credo. It does not permit Venezuela to cherry-pick which treaties or parts of treaties it observes or for what time – notwithstanding that it is one of the few countries in the world that has not actually signed the Convention. It cannot escape the demands of customary international law; but that non-signature sends clear signals. The 1897 Treaty of Washington and the Arbitration under it are sacred in terms of jurisdictional cover. Its mutual undertakings that the Award of the Tribunal of Arbitration shall be **'a full, perfect and final'** settlement is inviolable. It is not subject to a jurisdictional veto. That is why Guyana was there – to uphold its sacred rights of patrimony. And that is why Venezuela should have been there also, were its claims just. Characteristically, it tried to avoid the Court's proceedings.

It was unfortunate that Venezuela did not participate in the proceedings. It is, after all, an obligation of both Guyana and Venezuela to comply with the decision of the Secretary-General under the Geneva Agreement. What is clear, is that it is for the Court itself to determine whether it has jurisdiction. Otherwise, the principles underlying peaceful dispute settlement through judicial procedures would be seriously undermined. Guyana was ever confident that in choosing the principal judicial organ of the United Nations, the Secretary-General was acting consistent with his powers under the Geneva Agreement, and that by conferring such powers on the Secretary-General in 1966, Venezuela has consented to judicial settlement if the Court ultimately was his choice as the means of settlement – as it has been.

On 18th December 2020 the International Court of Justice gave its decision. It found, by twelve votes to four:

> "that it has jurisdiction to entertain the Application filed by the Cooperative Republic of Guyana on 29 March 2018 in so far as it concerns the validity of the Arbitral Award of 3 October 1899 and the related question of the definitive settlement of the land boundary dispute between the Cooperative Republic of Guyana and the Bolivarian Republic of Venezuela." (para. 138)
>
> Judgement of the ICJ – 18.12.2020

Shortly before the ICJ gave that decision on the issue of its jurisdiction to hear Guyana's case, a Venezuelan legal scholar, having argued against the Court's right to do so, ended his measured review with the following advice: [translated]

Whatever is the decision adopted by the Court in the jurisdictional phase, it would be irresponsible to call for its non-recognition by appealing to the patriotic sentiments of Venezuelans, as has unfortunately been the case over the last years, with the rulings of international tribunals that are not pleasing to those who control the reins of the country. Not honouring international compromises are not past Venezuelans' DNA. Unless someone has another solution, patriotism will continue defending Venezuela's rights, if necessary, even in the phase on the merits at the International Court of Justice, respecting the rules of the game, and accepting that, perhaps, we are not always right.

That, of course, was precisely what the Government of Venezuela did not do.

Venezuela's Outrage

The Court's decision appears to have inflamed the Venezuelan authorities. That is the all too common effect of law on lawlessness. President Maduro renounced the decision to the United Nations Secretary-General, to the Members of the UN Security Council and to the President of the Court itself. To the Chairman of the Caribbean Community, he condemned the decision as 'biased and irregular'. An official Communique of the Venezuelan Government described Guyana as *clinging to the fruitless mirage of unilateral judicial paths*. But Venezuela's outrage did not end there.

On January 7th, three weeks after the Court's judgement, the President of Venezuela, Mr Nicolas Maduro, trumpeted a Decree before his country's National Assembly (Decree No. 4415). In that tirade, President Maduro purported to establish a new maritime territory of Venezuela called the "Territory for the development of the Atlantic Façade". He claimed, for Venezuela, "sovereignty and exclusive sovereign rights in the waters and seabed adjacent to Guyana's coast, west of the Essequibo River".

Guyana's response was swift. It immediately advised its sister-states in the Caribbean Community (CARICOM) and the international community, including the Organization of American States (the OAS), the Commonwealth and the Organisation of African, Caribbean and Pacific States (the ACP) of the development. Support for Guyana was immediate. CARICOM Heads of Government, on January 12, publicly repudiated "any acts of aggression by Venezuela against Guyana". CARICOM leaders also reiterated their "firm and unswerving support for the maintenance and preservation of the sovereignty and territorial integrity of Guyana". Other nations, including the United States of America and Canada, also indicated their concern about this further threat to Guyana. A map appurtenant to the Decree is yet to be Gazetted in Caracas, but it might be instructive to see another map circulating there that followed another unilateral Maduro Decree (No.1,787).

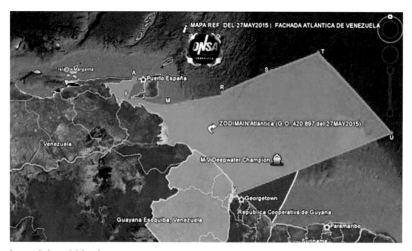

Imperial ambition!

And matters did not end there. On January 21st 2021, Guyana received distressing reports that a Venezuelan naval vessel had seized two Guyanese civilian fishing vessels – the *Lady Nayera* and the *Sea Wolf* – operating off the coast of Waini Point within Guyana's Exclusive Economic Zone. This incursion by Venezuelan armed forces into Guyana's Exclusive Economic Zone (EEZ) and its arrest and detention of the crews of Guyanese fishing boats was a flagrant violation of international law and the sovereign rights and jurisdiction of Guyana over its maritime spaces. The crews and the fishing vessels were detained by the Venezuelan military at Port Guiria in Venezuela, despite Guyana's formal protest to the Venezuelan authorities through diplomatic channels.

The Government of Guyana also immediately alerted the international community of this latest violation of international law by Venezuela and its illegal and arbitrary arrest and detention of Guyanese citizens in Guyana's waters. Guyana also registered to the Government of Venezuela its protest, in the strongest possible terms, at this unlawful and aggressive action against the State and people of Guyana, and insisted upon the immediate release and return of the two Guyanese vessels and their crews.

We are not Alone

On January 27th, CARICOM Heads of Government again publicly called on Venezuela to "desist from aggressive acts that will seriously undermine the peace and security not only of Guyana and Venezuela but the entire Caribbean region" and called "for the immediate release of the crew members and vessels".

The same day, the Organization of American States (OAS) condemned "the illegal detention" of the two Guyanese registered fishing vessels and their crew. It demanded the prompt and safe release of the crew and their boats and reiterated "its support for the rules and processes set by international law regarding ongoing territorial conflicts". The OAS emphasized that the resolution of the issue between Venezuela and Guyana *"is a matter that lies under international jurisdiction, and cannot be settled by unilateral actions"*. The Organization of 33 countries was clear that;

"any attempt to derail this international legal process, such as the decree issued by the Maduro regime, is contrary to international law and standards, and has no legal bearing or significance."

OAS General Secretariat (ref. E-004/21)

Following the active intervention of CARICOM leaders, the fishing vessels and their crew were released by Venezuela on 2nd February 2021. CARICOM's fraternity was particularly manifest in those days of threat. On 24th February 2021, at their 32nd Inter-Sessional Meeting, Heads of Government of CARICOM countries –

> *"welcomed the decision of the International Court of Justice ... that it had jurisdiction to entertain the Application filed by Guyana ... and noted that it paves the way for the ICJ to consider the merits of the case concerning the Arbitral Award of 3 October, 1899."*

Caricom leaders also

> *"expressed their disappointment over the rejection by Venezuela of the decision of the Court and its subsequent actions against Guyana including the issuance of Venezuelan Decree No.4415 on January 7, 2021, which claimed for Venezuela sovereignty and exclusive sovereign rights in the waters and sea-bed adjacent to Guyana's coast and the subsequent illegal interception and detention, in the Exclusive economic Zone of Guyana, of two Guyanese registered fishing vessels and their crew members by a Venezuelan naval vessel on January 21, 2021. They noted with satisfaction that the cumulative effort of the region contributed to the unconditional release by Venezuela of the fishing vessels and crews."*

As important as anything else, CARICOM leaders *expressed their full support for the ongoing judicial process that is intended to bring a peaceful and definitive end to the long-standing controversy between the two countries and urged Venezuela to participate in the process.* And to cap it all off they, *"affirmed their consistent support for the maintenance and preservation of the sovereignty and territorial integrity of Guyana."*

As Guyana's President, Dr Irfaan Ali, reminded Guyanese on 30th January 2021 in reporting on developments to date:

"We have friends. We are not alone. We have the international community behind us."

Guyana may need them. As has been written, Venezuela took its provocation to new heights – literally – shortly afterwards. On March 2, 2021 two Venezuelan Russian-made fighter jets overflew and circled the community and airstrip at Eteringbang, on the Guyana side of the border, at a threatening 1,500 feet altitude. Guyana condemned the overflight, declaring it an act of aggression and a violation of Guyana's sovereignty. Speaking in the National Assembly on 28th January 2021 Guyana's Foreign Minister protested:

"The incursion of our territory by the two Venezuelan fighter jets is a clear indication that the Government of Venezuela is prepared to use aggression and intimidation to accomplish what cannot be accomplished by legal means – the surrender by Guyana of its patrimony."

Despite it all, Guyana remains fully committed to the rule of international law and to the ICJ process. It is mindful that international law and independent international jurists of the highest calibre offer the most credible and definitive way in which to put an end to the Venezuelan contention.

Venezuela's Opposition to Legal Process

On the strategic front, in relation to its crusade to undo the 1899 Arbitral Award that fixed the boundary with Guyana, Venezuela has been opposed to legal process, and so to the International Court of Justice. They are fundamentally at odds with the process of 'judicial resolution', which they fear will go against them. From

1962, when they formally raised their 'claim' in the context of Guyana's Independence, to the present, Venezuela has pursued a tactic of pressure, hostility, aggression and filibuster to bully Guyana into a territorial settlement – 58 years of antagonism masquerading as peaceful 'reclamation'. In this, they have been mindful of the vast inequalities that have traditionally prevailed on almost every front.

This is why they opposed, and continue to resist, a judicial settlement. Their present tactic is to undo the ICJ process and replace it by 'friendly negotiations'. They saw a change of Government in Guyana in 2020 as an opportunity to reverse the judicial process already underway. In a Communique issued by the Government of Venezuela on 3rd August 2020, after saying that "Venezuela wishes to resume the bonds of cooperation and good neighbourliness, characteristic of the integral bilateral relation with Guyana until 2015," it concluded:

> "Lastly, in relation to the historic territorial controversy over the Guayana Essequibo, the Bolivarian Republic of Venezuela reiterates to the New Government of the Cooperative Republic of Guyana the need to reactivate, soonest, the mechanisms for dialogue and negotiations in order to arrive at a practical and satisfactory settlement, always within the framework of the 1966_Geneva Agreement, a valid international, legal instrument for both parties."

The Communique was an unashamed attempt to disrupt the ICJ process and go back to the 'good offices' process and Venezuela's old tactic of pressure and filibuster – as well as to avoid the possibility of a World Court judgement affirming the existing boundary – on Roraima. They were answered in President Ali's Inauguration Address. After alluding to the 2007 (PPP/C Government) settlement of the maritime boundary with Suriname through ITLOS, President Ali continued:

From President Irfaan Ali's Inauguration Address, 8th August 2020

"It was also a PPP/C Government in 2014 that put an end to the interminable 'good offices' dialogue with Venezuela, our neighbour to the West, because it had become, for them, a strategy for prolonging contention rather than seeking solution. Therefore, the PPP/C gave full support to the former administration when, as initiated by us, they submitted the Venezuela contention to the International Court of Justice.

In doing so, as a united people, Guyanese went to the top of the mountain of peace. We shall not descend. The sovereignty of our State, the integrity of our territory – of both land and sea – is a sacred trust. In being faithful to that trust, we shall be loyal to our enduring vision of Guyana as One Nation indivisible."

All Governments in Guyana have faced Venezuelan predatory challenges over the years of Independence: all Prime Ministers, all Presidents, all political parties, all the people of Guyana. And they have faced them in solidarity. The Opposition in Guyana's Parliament today is part of the country's advisory body on 'border' issues. And so has it been before. It is essential to Guyana's cause that it so continues. A united Guyana can be confident that it shall overcome these challenges on all fronts. Guyana's neighbours must know that they challenge a united Guyana. They must hear ringing across Guyana's borders the *Song of the Republic* sung with clear voice and from stout hearts:

From Pakaraima's peaks of pow'r
To Courantyne's lush sands,
Her children pledge each faithful hour
To guard Guyana's lands.
To foil the shock of rude invader
Who'd violate her earth
To cherish and defend forever
The State that gave them birth.

In the 59th year since Venezuela besmirched the name of their great Liberator by attempting to despoil the right to self-determination of the people of Guyana within their colonial domain, President Maduro feels too endangered by the rule of law. He fears the arm of international jurisprudence. He wants to end the judicial process to which Venezuela has been called. In Venezuela's sixtieth year of wrongdoing at Guyana's expense he wants to leave the path of justice and return to 'talks about talks'. Guyana will not oblige. The way forward is to The Hague.

The 'Justice' of the 1899 Award

A final word may be appropriate about the 'justice' of Guyana's cause – about the justice of its boundary from Punta Playa to the summit of Roraima and beyond to the Rupunnuni – the western boundary of the Essequibo region. It is important to remember that the boundary between Guyana and Venezuela has been twice the subject of intensive and extensive scrutiny at the highest level of erudition and integrity.

The Cleveland Commission

The first inquiry was by a high-level Commission appointed by the President of the United States – a Commission of enquiry to "investigate and report upon the true divisional line between the Republic of Venezuela and British Guiana". It was appointed by President Cleveland in 1896 in the name of the 'Munroe Doctrine' in defiance of Britain's refusal to agree to an arbitral process with Venezuela. The members of the Commission were all distinguished. Its Chairman was David J, Brewer, an Associate Justice of the Supreme Court of the United States and it included among its members Andrew D. White, a founder of Cornell University and an eminent historian and diplomat.

The American Commission was 'non-adversarial'; but both Venezuela and Britain made elaborate written submissions to it. The report of the US Commission listed its publications as 4 volumes of its own, including an atlas of 76 maps, 5 British 'Blue Books', 3 volumes of Venezuelan documents, and a historical account from the Venezuelan Government

The Commission worked assiduously throughout 1896; but negotiations were continuing with Britain over 'binding arbitration' and on 12 November, 1896, the 'Agreement between Venezuela and Great Britain and the United States of America on a Proposed Treaty of Arbitration between Great Britain and Venezuela' was signed by Britain and the United States in Washington. In the event, although the Cleveland Commission had done massive work, and was within sight of a decision, its activities were terminated with the prospect of binding Arbitration in sight.

The Treaty of Washington followed the next year (1897) between Britain and Venezuela. As elaborated earlier (see, p. 19) the Treaty established an Arbitral Tribunal of extraordinarily high judicial quality. In the quest for justice, a more illustrious membership would be hard to conceive.

The 'Paris' Tribunal

If the labours of the American Commission were extensive, those of the Arbitral Tribunal under the Treaty of Washington were even more so – particularly since Venezuela and Britain were directly represented before it. The fact that Venezuela placed the origin of its claim in a Papal Bull of 1493 is indicative of what faced the Tribunal in its examination of the history of occupation of the territory. The arguments in Paris – where the Tribunal met –went on for nearly three months. The verbatim records of the hearings occupy 54 printed volumes.

In all of this, the Tribunal went over the ground just covered by the US Commission – perhaps going a bit deeper and further. But the mandate and the mission were the same, On 3 March 1897 the *New York Times* made the point that the US Commission had "in effect, done the work of the Tribunal for it in advance, and in this way has rendered even a more important service than it was appointed to render to **the cause of justice and the cause** of peace".

Article I of the Treaty of Washington required that *An Arbitral Tribunal shall be immediately appointed to determine the boundary-line between the Colony of British Guiana and the United States of Venezuela* and by Article XIII Britain and Venezuela agreed to consider the proceeds of the Tribunal *as a full, perfect and final settlement of all the questions referred to the Arbitrators.*

A Unanimous Decision

The decision of the Tribunal was unanimous, and in his closing Statement after the Award was read President de Martens stressed that unanimity was the paramount achievement of the Tribunal. The parties, he said, *had the satisfaction of having unanimity among the arbitrators on all aspects of the Award, without any reservation whatsoever.* The London *Times* the following day reported him as saying:

> **From the London *Times* of 4 October 1899:**
>
> *"The boundary line which has been laid down by the judges* is **a line based on justice and law.** *The judges have been actuated by a desire to establish a compromise in a very complicated question, the origin of which must be looked for at the end of the 15th century."*

A line based on justice and law! A good test of that claim would be to compare it with the only similar attempt to determine the boundary – the work of the Cleveland Commission four years earlier – the first time the boundary had been adjudged *in justice and law.* We have seen how the Commission was terminated, rightly, in favour of the international 'binding' Tribunal under the Treaty of Washington; but the mandate was the same; the search was the same. How did the likely finding of the Cleveland Commission compare with what later emerged from the 'Paris' Tribunal? The closer they are, the more likely they are to be just; the more likely the boundary line to be right in law.

Venezuelan 'Injustice'

The so called "injustice" of the boundary line awarded by the 1899 Tribunal is basic to the Venezuelan claim. After 63 years of accepting, recognizing and protecting the line the Tribunal laid down, it was to its 'injustice' that Venezuela turned in 1962 in its effort to frustrate Guyana's self-determination with its territory intact. Through all the years since then, it is that 'injustice' Caracas has pleaded – whether deriving from false claims of British dishonesty with maps, or the Tribunal's 'compromises', or the Mallet-Prevost 'fable' – it is to the resulting 'injustice' of the boundary line that Venezuela appeals. It was so in the Decolonisation Committee in 1962. It is so today. On 7 January, 2021, President Maduro wrote to the UN Secretary-General of *"the unfortunate, fraudulent" and illegal 1899 Arbitral Award"*. The same day, the Government of Venezuela's Communique spoke of *"the grotesque fraud of the 1899 Award"*. The people of Venezuela have been fed the cultivated falsehood that they have been the victim of the 'injustice' of the 1899 Award.

And recalling 1962, when Venezuela tried to convince the United States of its 'innocence; in interrupting Guyana's independence process, it was for; justice' that it appealed.

> *"Venezuela was not questioning the legality of the Arbitral Award.*
> *... Venezuela considers the Award to have been inequitable and questionable from a moral point of view,"*
>
> Walter Brandt to the US State Department (see, p.31 above)

'Justice' twice fulfilled

At the very end of the Meade Report (1963) – the British Expert's Report in response to the Report of the Venezuelan Experts post 1962 – is the following:

> *"And the last words may be left to Mr. A.D. White, who had been a member of the U.S. Venezuelan Boundary Commission appointed by President Cleveland in 1896. Although it carried out its investigations during the 1896 and its reports are contained in many volumes it was*

dissolved after the signing of the Arbitration Treaty and before it stated its view as to the boundary line. The following quotation is therefore the only indication of any conclusions reached by the Commission of which it will be remembered. Judge Brewer was President and Mr. Mallet-Prevost was Secretary. After stating that he believes the 1899 award to be 'thoroughly just' Mr. White adds:

It is with pride and satisfaction that I find their award agreeing, substantially, with the line which, after so much trouble, our own Commission had worked out."

It has now become possible to examine Mr White's important words more thoroughly. Who was he, first of all? As indicated earlier, he was a distinguished historian and diplomat; the co-founder of Cornell University and later President of the US delegation to the 1899 Hague Peace Conference. He had worked hard as a member of the Cleveland Commission and was fully prepared to be critical of the British where he saw fit. Above all, he was a man of palpable integrity. Below, is a quote from Vol. 2 of Mr White's 'Autobiography' speaking to the 'justice' of the 1899 Arbitral Award:

"One former prime minister of Great Britain I learned, during this investigation to respect greatly, – Lord Aberdeen, whom I well-remembered as discredited and driven from power ... Since that time his wisdom has, I think, been recognized, and I am now glad to acknowledge the fact that of all the many British statesmen who dealt with the Venezuelan question, he was clearly the most just. The line he drew seemed to me the fairest possible. He did not attempt to grasp the mouth of the Orinoco, nor did he meander about choice gold-fields or valuable strategic points, seeking to include them. The Venezuelans themselves had shown willingness to accept his proposal; but alleged, as their reason for not doing so, that

the British government had preached to them regarding their internal policy so offensively that self-respect forbade them to acquiesce in any part of it.

Toward this Aberdeen line we tended more and more, and in the sequel we heard, with very great satisfaction, that the Arbitration Tribunal at Paris had practically adopted this line, **which we of the commission had virtually agreed upon.** *It need hardly be stated that, each side having at the beginning of the arbitration claimed the whole vast territory between the Orinoco and the Essequibo, neither was quite satisfied with the award. But I believe it to be thoroughly just, and that it forms a most striking testimony of the value of international arbitration in such questions, as a means, not only of preserving international peace, but of* **arriving at substantial justice.**

... Never, before that award, did any of us, I am sure, indicate to any person what our view as to the line between the possessions of Venezuela and Great Britain was; but now we may do so, and I feel that all concerned may be congratulated on the fact that **two tribunals, each seeking to do justice, united on the same line, and that line virtually the same which one of the most just of British statesmen had approved many years before.**

It should be as Mr Meade had said: 'the last word' on the 'justice' of the Award. The American Commission set up in defiance of the British refusal to go to formal arbitration, under the Chairmanship of a Judge of the US Supreme Court, with the best of experts at its command, and after voluminous and meticulous research, reaches toward a conclusion on the line of the boundary between British Guiana and Venezuela that is substantially the same as that later awarded by the 1899 Arbitral Tribunal. A line which 122 years later the Government of Venezuela describes as a 'grotesque fraud'.

The 1899 Arbitral Tribunal did its own work; and because it had done it as thoroughly as its predecessor it came to substantially the same conclusion. The boundary line it found and decreed is substantially that which the US Commission had reached. Twice has that line been examined and explored with integrity and the highest scholarship available; and each time the answer has been the same. The 'injustice' lies in the shameful quest of falsity that Venezuela has cultivated and pursued to the devastating point of self-belief.